Michael Winicott

TEN REASONS WHY
BILL GATES
IS RICHER THAN YOU

10 REASONS YOU COULD CASH IN TO IMPROVE YOUR WEALTH

© 2015 by Sarah Retter

© 2015 by UNITEXTO

Published by UNITEXTO

UNITEXTO
Digital Publishing

TABLE OF CONTENTS

INTRODUCTION

This book is going to share some key reasons to Bill Gates' success. He is an unmistakable American entrepreneur, investor, philanthropist with a terrific success in the development of software for personal-computers.

The life story of Bill Gates explains why he is one of the richest individuals on Earth.

Gates has been No. 1 for many years on the Bloomberg Billionaires List, until Carlos Slim Helu took No. 1 spot in 2010. Also, in May 2013, with a fortune of $72 billion Bill Gates turned into the richest man on the planet again and retook the world's richest title from Carlos Slim. Bill Gates' total assets was $79.3 billion as of April 09, 2015.

But his early life dumbstruck all. Gates was expelled from the second year in Harvard University. Inconvenience turned to subsequent success. At school, he had serious problems with Grammar, Citizenship and other subjects, which he considered banal. For bad behavior in elementary school, Gates was sent to a psychiatrist.

But still, how did he reach so far?

So, continue reading until the end of the book and change your life for the better...

BRIEF INSIGHT INTO BILL GATES'S LIFE.

William Henry Gates III (Bill) was born on October 28, 1955, in Seattle, Washington. Bill was the second of three children in an upper-middle class family. He delighted in playing games with the family and was exceptionally focused. He additionally loved to read. Bill got to be exhausted in public school so his family sent him to Lakeside School, a private school, where he exceeded expectations in math and science and did well in drama and English.

Gates got to be interested in PC programming when he was 13, amid the time of huge mainframe PCs. His school held a fund raiser to buy a print terminal so students could utilize PC time that was given by General Electric. Using this time, Gates composed a tic-tac-toe program using BASIC, one of the first computer languages. Later he made a PC version of Risk, a prepackaged game he preferred in which the objective is global control.

At Lakeside, Bill met Paul Allen, who shared his enthusiasm for PCs. Gates and Allen and two different students hacked into a PC fitting in with Computer Center Corporation (CCC) to get free PC time however were gotten. After a time of probation, they were permitted back in the PC lab when they offered to settle glitches in CCC's software. At age 17, Gates and Allen were paid $20,000 for a system called Traf-O-Data that was utilized to tally traffic.

In mid-1973, Bill Gates served as a congressional page in the U.S. Place of Representatives. He scored 1590 out of 1600 on the SAT and was acknowledged by Harvard University. Steve Ballmer, who got to be CEO of Microsoft after Bill retired, was additionally a Harvard student. Meanwhile, Paul Allen dropped out of Washington College to take a shot at PCs at Honeywell Corporation and persuaded Gates to drop out of Harvard and go along with him in beginning another software organization in Albuquerque, New Mexico. They called it Micro-Soft. This was soon changed to Microsoft, and they moved their organization to Bellevue, Washington.

In 1980, IBM, one of the biggest technology organizations of the time, requested that Microsoft write software to run their new personal PC, the IBM PC. Microsoft kept the licensing rights for the operating system (MS-DOS) with the goal that they earned money for each PC sold first by IBM, and later by the various organizations that made PC computers. Microsoft developed rapidly from 25 employees in 1978 to more than 90,000 today.

Throughout the years, Microsoft created many new advancements and some of the world's most well-known software and products, for example, Word and Power Point. Even though some have condemned Gates for using faulty business practices, he incorporated Microsoft with one of the biggest organizations on the planet. He has been portrayed as splendid yet childlike, driven, aggressive, extreme, fun, yet ailing in compassion.

Bill Gates is one of the richest men on the planet. In 2012, his $61 billion dollars in resources made him the world's second richest man according to Forbes Magazine. In 2006, Gates reported that he would reduce his association at Microsoft to invest more energy in philanthropy. The Bill and Melinda Gates Foundation supports the mission to destroy Polio, to fight AIDS, jungle fever and tuberculosis; to give inoculations to children; and so many other initiatives.

THE 10 MOST IMPORTANT SUCCESS REASONS FOR BILL GATES

The prevalent misconception is that Bill Gates is a visionary. He foresaw his MS-DOS operating system as a goldmine, and he hoodwinked IBM, the greatest computer organization on earth, into giving him a chance to hold the copyright. Microsoft programming still commands the desktop over 30 years after Gates propelled the personal computer revolution.

This story fits with the generally held thought that surfacing with a "major thought" is what it takes to fulfill a great deal, and turn out to be exceptionally affluent.

The most fruitful, the ones who have turned out to be immensely rich, know better. All say that success requires phenomenal execution on a standard thought.

In reality, if you look all the more carefully at the subtle elements of Bill Gates' entrepreneurial life, you'll see it underpins the last point, as well.

Gates took Microsoft to the top by executing splendidly, and dependably in service of other individuals' visions, never his own. By parlaying his way through a progression of ever-greater business bargains -all with genuinely normal products- he went from zero to billions in under 10 years.

Here are the 10 basic ways Bill Gates aced execution.

1. Powerful Partnerships

Gates was never proud of making it impossible to be the second banana. Like a genuine business visionary, Gates saw the "structural holes" in the personal computing marketplace and moved into occupy them, generally in a subordinate spot to the huge players.

First Gates located Microsoft as the junior partner to the pioneering MITS, and afterward served in a comparable junior-partner role with industry pioneer Digital Research. The minimal known version of Microsoft's marriage to IBM is that Gates began as a fervent intermediary between Digital Research and IBM. Gates keenly attempted to unite the two mammoths, content to be the second class software in a marriage between big players.

In any case, when Digital Research and IBM couldn't get married, Gates ventured into the void, expecting that IBM may stop the PC extend through and through. Regardless, Gates regarded IBM's potential force in the PC market and needed to be a part of it.

The incongruity is that when Gates had gone ahead to wind up the richest man on earth, the first two of his "senior" partners were a distant memory and forgotten. The third, IBM, stopped making PCs in 2004.

Also, incidentally, Gates never hoodwinked his partner IBM into giving him a chance to keep the licensing rights to MS-DOS. IBM's policy was to not hold the rights for any product created outside its entryways, inspired by a paranoid fear of legal risk. Gates got the same arrangement on licensing that IBM would have given to Digital Research or any other individual.

Train your new CEO

If you're a smart inquisitive individual it can be painful to run an organization of more than 50 individuals. You invest more energy than you'd like repeating yourself, sitting in exhausting meetings, skimming over long authoritative reports in which you know there are blunders, and so on. The allurement is to give over control to the first "expert manager" who tags along.

What's more, that's what the standard investor formula directs. In any case, Bill Gates didn't do that. He hired Steve Ballmer in 1980 and gave him the CEO job 20 years after the fact. Profiting in the product products business requires domain skill and a pledge to taking care of issues within that domain. Extraordinary tech organizations are at times worked by non-specialized management or expert managers.

Adobe is another great case. The two organizers were PhD computer science researchers from Xerox PARC who were enthusiastic about taking care of issues in the publishing and graphics world. They are still directing operations at Adobe.

Note that this is a rule that Old Economy organizations have long caught on. Jack Welch joined GE in 1961 and got to be CEO 20 years after the fact. Sometimes an Old Economy organization might pull in a couple of outsiders to senior positions be that as it may, in light of the fact that they have such stable administrations underneath, they can more effortlessly afford this than startups.

2. Strategic Acting

Now you may be thinking about how is the strategy applicable to amassing riches or getting to be fruitful. I would say that it is absolutely pivotal as it is strategy that helps you to go straightaway for the execution and not get occupied by different facts.

Simple arranging will totally fall level if not joined by the right strategy and business order to position it viably. How about we examine Microsoft's tie up with Digital Research. It was the main producer of working programming for PCs at that time. First they marketed an interpreter that could help Digital research programming to be utilized on Apple computer and after that when IBM needed a working programming for its new PC venture, Bill Gates volunteered.

By chance this maybe is one of the greatest breaks in their prosperity diagram. Microsoft got the chance to commence their business destined for success. More than skill and arranging, it was sheer positioning that

Bill Gates was to gain by his ability and make millions from the popular MS DOS for IBM computers.

The way that Bill Gates perceived IBM's potential in the PC industry and chose to play on it with the right position is maybe what was instrumental in wrapping everything up for them and guaranteeing a solid platform to begin off their major achievement trail, one of the century's greatest.

Instead of only developing or dreaming, Gates took a restrained approach toward software as a potential source of business opportunities.

He and his partner Paul Allen composed the first form of Microsoft BASIC just to get in on the ground floor with a pioneer creator of home-built PC units. Gates quit Harvard and moved to New Mexico to work with the organization, named MITS, hoping to make Microsoft BASIC an industry standard.

A couple of years after the fact, Gates and Allen made comparable moves to draw near to Digital Research, then the main producer of the most prominent PC operating system. They even marketed an interpreter that permitted Digital Research software to chip away at Apple PCs, as a vital move to ride on Digital Research's coattails.

Microsoft's binds to Digital Research drove directly to its huge open door, with IBM. At the point when IBM couldn't get Digital Research to give an operating system to IBM's new PC venture, Gates arrived to volunteer for the job. It didn't make a difference that Microsoft had no ability in operating systems.

Strategic positioning, and in addition a little good fortune -not some "huge thought"- gave Gates the chance to make billions with MS-DOS for IBM.

3. Fierce Tenacity

This particular truth is best stated in Bill Gates' own words,

"Do the right things, long enough, consistently."

Imagine the enormous misfortune this entire world would have endured if Bill Gates abandoned his drive the first time he confronted an issue or notwithstanding when he was ousted from Harvard? Regardless of his ability, splendor in execution, the world would have passed up a great opportunity for a great product on the grounds that the individual, who was enhancing, did not hold up sufficiently long or rather surrendered too early.

Achievement does not arrive in a platter. One needs to make progress toward it, work towards it and achieve it a tiny bit at a time. Not at all like what you see, it is never an overnight move. There is no pixie Godmother whose enchantment wand helps you awaken a mogul subsequent to spending the night as a poor person.

Almost like a bit of earth on a potter's wheel, achievement needs mind, sustaining and above all persistence to bear fruit. Unless you have that key component, you will never have the capacity to achieve all the great dreams that you may have spun in your mind. The relentlessness, to hold tight even notwithstanding hostile condition, is what sees you through the last lap of this game.

Gates dependably offered his partners some assistance with succeeding on their terms, not his own. With MS-DOS, timing was IBM's vital concern. Missed due dates may bring about IBM higher-ups to pull the plug on the PC venture, yet Microsoft had only a couple of months to deliver the software. So Microsoft took a no fuss easy route. It purchased the rights to a PC operating system made by another Seattle software organization, and based MS-DOS on top of it. Gates later let it be known would have taken a year for Microsoft to make MS-DOS starting with no outside help.

IBM was famously hard on its merchants. Amid the development period of MS-DOS, buttoned-down IBM officials harassed Microsoft employees on security breaches and minimal procedural points of interest. It drove Gates' colleagues nuts and they contrasted working with IBM with "riding the bear." But Gates continued and told his group to suck it up. MS-DOS was conveyed on time.

At first, the software was buggy to the point that IBM engineers needed to rewrite the whole thing. Be that as it may, the fact of the matter is that Gates did what the partner required. It didn't make a difference if MS-DOS was a disgraceful operating system in light of someone else's design. It came in on time and safeguarded the venture. As opposed to vision, and surely not pride of workmanship, Gates was about execution.

4. Guts

Bill was exceptionally energetic about computer programming. In this manner, as a student at Lakeside Prep School, he spent his days and evenings designing and composing computer projects. Expectedly, this took a substantial toll on his scholastic performance, as classes were skipped and homework left undone.

At the Computer Center Corporation, Bill and his companions slammed the system a few times and even sabotaged the security system, all in their enthusiastic mission to procure new computer skills. Yet, when they hacked into and modified the calculation that recorded computer usage time, they were quickly banned for a few weeks!

Confidence in one's capacity is essential for achievement. By confidence, we mean the capacity to dream, as well as the capacity to take it forward as opposed to suffocating in self-uncertainty. Maybe the first venture, that Bill Gates attempted best, exemplifies this trademark in him.

When he reached the then supervisors of the most recent micro PC, Altair 8800, about an essential mediator for platform, neither he nor his companion had composed any code for it and they had not in any case set their eyes on the new machine. Notwithstanding, that one thing, that took them forward, was the conviction that they could execute if they got the open door.

Sometimes opportunities don't just drop by yet you have to get them just like Bill Gates did from MITS. At the point when the MITS chief revealed intrigue and requesting that they demonstrate the product in couple of weeks, they had the guts again to accept and walk forth. They added to a model and in the long run even had an effective show. That goes ahead to demonstrate that it is so imperative to have that one of a kind quality in character to have confidence in your capacities and push ahead without self-uncertainty and anxiety blurring your achievements.

5. Integrity

On the other hand, guts alone may demonstrate inadequate if you don't back it up with a couple of more characteristics. Honesty and respectability in a specific order occupy pole position. Bill Gates did not rest by just reaching MITS. He additionally had the trustworthiness of character to convey what he guaranteed. A ton of times we hear about guarantees, yet the genuine element, that makes them worthwhile, is the manner by which effectively you can implement it.

While still at school, Bill and three of his partners setup a group called the Lakeside Programmers, on whose platform they hit an arrangement with Computer Center Corporation. The group reviewed computer projects to identify bugs and different issues. For this they were permitted boundless computer usage time at the Center. In his own words "It was the point at which we got free time at the Computer Center that we really got into computers..."

Next, the Lakeside Programmers were hired by Information Science Incorporated to make a payroll program. For this they again got free computer time and also commercial offers for the product.

What's more, for another organization called Traf-O-Data, Bill and his companion Allen made a product that measures traffic stream. This earned them about $20,000.

Under Microsoft Corporation, Bill gave the world the operating system programming called WINDOWS. Put conservatively, WINDOWS keeps running in more than sixty percent of all computers on planet earth! Bill gave the world awesome products and services, and was extraordinarily compensated.

Knowledge or achievement without uprightness can never positively affect your general achievement, and even your level of achievement is directly corresponding to the level of trustworthiness that you have towards your work.

Uprightness alone assumes a urgent part in securing a level of flawlessness and pushing you to convey your best in any given condition or circumstance without any other source of encouragement or driving force to perform second to none. It is this nature fueled independently from anyone else the inspiration that gives you the edge between an average product and a market champ.

Through his published books, Bill keeps on sharing so as to increase knowledge and improve the world. His wisdom and ideas; through his products and services, keep on enhancing our lives; and through the Bill and Melinda Gates Foundation, he keeps on giving his money away to favor and uplift humanity. What an awesome approach to serve God and Man.

Bill Gates will dependably be recalled, not for what he took out of the world for himself, yet for what he provided for the Universe.

6. Dynamism

This is another key trait that frequently recognizes a pioneer and an achiever from rest of the pack. It is the dynamism in their achievement. Bill Gates trusted that the predominance of his content will drive the interest for it, and he strived to achieve this prevalence by upgrading the dynamism in his content.

Content marketing as a business strategy was exclusively spearheaded by Bill Gates but rather what he included is a key impetus, and that is 'dynamism'. The dynamic content that he hawked in the market place combined with his honesty and high level of responsibility worked in making it an undisputable lord in the market.

Humanity most prominent advances are the ones that level the playing field.

Bill Gates has a solid conviction that "All lives have equal value." Help those that can't help themselves. Everyone merits a chance taking care of business life. Lift the underdogs of the world up.

In his speech at Harvard, Bill said, "I cleared out Harvard with no real consciousness of the dreadful imbalances on the planet. The appalling variations of wellbeing, riches and opportunities that sentenced a large number of individuals to lives of misery. I learned a considerable measure here at Harvard about new thoughts and financial aspects, and politics. I got incredible exposure to the advances being in the sciences. Be that as it may, humanity most noteworthy advances are not in its disclosures, but rather in how those revelations are applied to lessen disparity."

There is a sign on many entryways at Microsoft. It reads:

"Change the world, or go home"

Not just does that expression encapsulate a great many good intentions but identifies with the way Bill Gates drives his life. He lives to build a superior world, whether it's one adaptation, one platform, one system, one thought, one reason, one innovation at a time. The magnificence is that he knows how act and amplify his effect in capable ways: he's on top of his game.

7. Impromptu creation

It goes without saying that this is an essential component in all kinds of different contexts and particularly in the context of what you do and how you perform in life. The example of overcoming adversity of Bill Gates' life bears confirmation to the need to be creative by impulse.

At certain times impromptu creation works better in achieving an objective over years of flawlessness. In spite of the fact that it may seem like a peculiarity, the examples of overcoming adversity of any semblance of Bill Gates go ahead to clarify this splendidly. One of the key parts of Bill Gates' prosperity is likewise the way he is a business visionary past brilliance, and that is inconceivable without timely impromptu creation. Life is not really a textbook and never advances according to an arrangement, some extemporaneous out of the container thinking is an absolute need most times.

Bill Gates began his college education at Harvard in 1973, however needed to drop out in 1975 to put everything in order. With his companion Paul Allen, he setup Microsoft Corporation in 1975.

He dropped out of Harvard, not for absence of limit for higher education, but rather in light of the fact that his heart was not in his studies. Bill was so dedicated to his DREAM that he declined to be occupied even by the charm of formal education at the prestigious Harvard University!

8. Driven By Passion and Commitment

Enthusiasm almost always goes before achievement, yet achievement may not generally follow after energy. Yes, you read it right. The fact that Bill Gates had a gift for PCs and software is a known reality, yet imagine what might have happened if he overlooked it in light of a legitimate concern for his formal education?

Bill Gates as a Lakeside Prep School student spent many days designing PC programs. In spite of the fact that this implied that his scholastic performance suffered and his homework was deficient, he stayed focused on his energy.

Indeed, even later at Computer Center Corporation, many times Bill Gates and his companions wound up crashing the system in their drive to learn more PC skills. They were even banned for the whole summer for hacking into the system and changing its complete programming. Be that, as it may, it was for the better in the long run.

At the point when your enthusiasm drives your efforts, the level of responsibility additionally increases multiplying your effort and execution without it harming by any means. Therefore, duty and energy are similar to these effortlessly inflammable burning impetus that don't just arouse the flame of achievement and entrepreneurship, but additionally help in the final fulfillment of your dreams.

Splendid Execution

If you track the example of overcoming adversity of Microsoft opposite its associates, you will see that two of its greatest rivals are no more in business and the other one IBM, maybe the greatest among the group, has stopped making PCs.

Why did this happen? It is on the grounds that Bill Gates designed the ideal product as well as perceived the need to execute the arrangement. If Microsoft did not achieve the level of customer fulfillment that has now, it would not have been so successful: Companies and individuals in every continent and culture would never have received it with open arms if the performance of the product did not meet expectations. The amazing features of the Windows Operating System bear affirmation to this key truth.

9. Beginning Early

It is certain you more likely than not heard the many truisms that elaborate on the advantages of being an early bird to reap the maximum benefit. Maybe this additionally elaborates a central element that in spite of the given circumstance and accessibility of talent, why some succeed over others in achieving the same objective.

Think of the time Bill Gates began. Born in 1955, Bill's first contact with the computer was in 1968, at a young age of 13. He was then exploring different avenues regarding the many PC applications that later on would turn into the establishment of his inevitable achievement. Given how costly PCs were by then, he utilized his school PC widely by then of time to further his enthusiasm and offer shape to his dreams.

The way that he decided to usefully offer shape to his considerations instead of negligible daydreaming was what in the end turned the tide to support him.

Have a sense of urgency.

The world changes quick. The market changes quicker. Bill says, "In this business, when you realize you're stuck in an unfortunate situation, it's past the point where it is possible to spare yourself. Unless you're running frightened constantly, you're gone."

Pioneer the trail.

The way isn't generally there. It requires time to pick the right track. Sometimes you need to make it. Sometimes individuals will think you're insane. Sometimes you are just ahead of the bend. it's a dream for a reason, and sometimes making your dreams happen takes putting it all out there. Bill Gates trusted that the personal computer was the future and that there ought to be one on each desktop and in the family room and it would change the way we work and how we live in unbelievable ways.

10. Advancing the Knowledge Pool

Bill Gates, the person who we relate with accomplishment regardless of formal education is one of the best advocates of knowledge. A Co-director of the Bill Gates Foundation, he feels education is the best impetus that can change the course of a country and person. He proceeded with the mission to redesign the traditional scholarly practices to minimize dropouts and sharpen talents to accomplish one's objective.

Knowledge has no limits and there is no restriction to the amount you can learn and there is no knowledge that goes waste. It generally offers an individual some assistance with bringing out the best.

Your best shows signs of improvement with the right individuals in the nearby.

You're better when you have the highly qualified persons around you. Bill Gates fabricated a culture of the best and brightest and was great at persuading his companions, for example, Paul Allen and Steve Ballmer to go along with him on his experiences. By encompassing himself with brilliant individuals, Bill could scale.

He likewise had a sounding board for thoughts. All the more significantly, thoughts could show signs of improvement from the joined smarts and viewpoints. Bill additionally knows how to supplement his qualities by having the right individuals around that make up for his shortcomings.

Innovation is the absolute entirety of a business.

It's about putting up thoughts for sale to the public and applying research. If you don't innovate you die. The world continues evolving. To stay ahead of the game, or even to stay in the game, you need to continue enhancing: innovate in your products, innovate in your procedure, innovate in the markets, and so on. Bill Gates utilizes innovation as an approach to drive sway whether it's forming programming or sparing the planet.

Be the platform.

Be the platform individuals can build on. See the part that you play in building something for other individuals to build on what you excel at.

Build a superior system.

Don't just take care of a coincidental issue. Make the solution systematic and make it repeatable. Discover, make, or leverage systems. There is dependably a system, whether it's at the micro-level or the full scale level. The system has inputs and outputs, cycles, and levers. Whether you're making the system or utilizing the system, you're more powerful when you realize that there is a system.

Build an ecosystem.

There are systems and ecosystems surrounding us. Bill says, "Personal computing today is a rich ecosystem encompassing huge PC-based data centers, notebook and Tablet PCs, handheld gadgets, and savvy mobile phones. It has extended from the desktop and the data centers to wherever individuals need it — at their work areas, in a meeting, out and about or even noticeable all around." On making partners for your ecosystem, Bill says, "Our prosperity has really been founded on partnerships from the earliest starting point."

CONCLUSION

Maybe a single statement is never adequate to understand a singular achievement and its connection to the masses. Bill Gates' example of overcoming adversity is wonderful not just in view of the many millions he has earned but on how he can give it back to society what he has earned

What is give is what you get is the motto.

It additionally highlights a key lesson that we hopefully can learn. Accomplishments without the human touch and the need to give back the favors that you get in life is unimaginable. The egotistical could earn riches, however the philanthropist delivers the example of social behavior.

The greatness of prosperity is frequently aligned not by the amount earned but instead by the degree you are prepared to give back what you receive.

To have the capacity to see your prosperity as a gift that can and should be shared will only drive you to greater achievements and more success.

Also, for being such a beautiful motivation to our people, we say: Thank you Bill!

THE END